THE SCIENCE OF MIND WAY

THE SCIENCE OF MIND WAY
...to Success, Wealth & Love

A Simple Guide to Understanding
the Basic Concepts of Science of Mind
and How They Can Jump-Start Your Life

Joan McCall

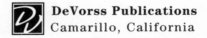

DeVorss Publications
Camarillo, California

The Science of Mind Way
Copyright ©2014 by Joan McCall

"Science of Mind" is a registered U.S. trademark of SOMARK, Inc., and all rights are reserved. Permission has been granted by United Centers for Spiritual Living, Golden CO. For more information, please visit its website at: www.unitedcentersforspiritualliving.org

Library of Congress Control Number: 2014957566
ISBN13: 978-0-87516-877-7
FIRST PRINTING, 2015

DeVorss & Company, Publisher
P.O. Box 1389
Camarillo, CA 93011-1389
www.devorss.com

Printed in the United States of America

TABLE OF CONTENTS

TABLE OF CONTENTS

A Word from the Author

As a television screenwriter in my early career days, my job was full of changes, edits, rewrites, and crumpled up sheets of paper on the floor. In television, creating the perfect relationship or the improbable rags-to-riches story was as simple as typing the dialogue that ultimately leads to the happy ending. But as I grew spiritually, I soon came to realize that real life doesn't quite work that way. Something deeper was pushing me to understand the source of my experiences, my thoughts, my words and how they shaped my personal reality.

I had already had some success because I expected good things to happen for me. But later, I began to soak up the negativity of others and lost confidence in myself. That's when my career all but dried up. You see, I believed that God wanted the best for me and that's what happened . . . until it didn't happen anymore. I grew depressed and hopeless until one day,

I opened *The Science of Mind* by Ernest Holmes and read, "What thought can do, it can undo." After fifteen years of studying and practicing metaphysics, one day the light turned on in my head as I finally understood exactly what was creating my experiences. I was shaken by that thought . . . awestruck even.

The Science of Mind taught me about a life principle that anyone can use to free themselves from life's ills and problems. Here is a principle that will create healthy, loving relationships, a prosperous lifestyle, and peace of mind. What is this principle? It is the law of life, the way experiences come into being. Far from being helpless creatures existing in a dog-eat-dog, survival-of-the-fittest world, we are rulers of our own personal universe.

The way I was thinking and feeling had everything to do with the quality of my life, from my career to my relationships to my bank account. I had grown to expect less, and less is what I got. Now that I believed I had found the secret to life, I started to work with it. Accepting and committing to the life principle was tough work at first because I had fallen into the trap of negativity. As my mother used to say, "I was down so low I had to reach up to touch bottom." So I started to write down what I wished my life to be. And slowly I began to demonstrate better conditions. I was led to start a whole new career that is flourishing to this day. At the same time I became a minister and started teaching this principle and watched it work miracles for others.

This little book holds the key to success. As a minister, so often people would come up to me after a service and explain "their" problem and "their" story, hoping for some guidance and a quick solution. We all know there's no quick solution. But this book is a quick step in the right direction. It will spark the energy in you to look deeper and understand the life principle that will in fact provide the solution you're looking for. It contains the principle. You can work it as well as anyone, including me. I wrote it for you. All you have to do is speak the words with belief and power.

Joan McCall
Los Angeles, California

God gives some more than others,

because some accept more than others.

— ERNEST HOLMES

CHAPTER 1

Seeds for Success

———•◦•———

From ancient wisdom to the pop culture of today, the world has contemplated and believed in the concept of planting seeds for success. In the fifth century it was Buddhist monk Bodhidharma who said, "If we should be blessed by some great reward, such as fame or fortune, it's the fruit of a seed planted by us in the past." Now consider that next to a twenty-first-century pop star like Katy Perry, who says, "I think we're all blessed with gifts. I was lucky I just found out what my gift was early on and have planted that seed and tried to water it every day." The Science of Mind Way starts from within. Planting a seed is our first step. Let's take a look at the role we play in our own success.

Every single person in the world is born with gifts and talents. Many of us are aware of those talents quite early in our lives. But many of us — even far into adulthood — still don't know what our talents are. And because of this we set very few goals. Maybe we also don't achieve very much. It seems like life keeps on handing us crumbs from that great banquet table of life that we see in the distance.

Most of us have set goals and some of us have even achieved them. Most people set reasonable goals that they believe are pretty easy to achieve. But not many people set big, unreasonable goals. Why not? Because they don't think they can achieve them. They are just dreams. They're so big, so risky, and they require too much money and time and effort to realize them.

Gary Ryan Blair, in his book *Goals: The 10 Rules for Achieving Success*, says that "Goals are the seeds of success — you become only what you plant."

Well, I don't believe we become our goals. We experience them. A goal is an idea we'd like to experience. Setting a goal is the beginning of the creation of that experience. A goal operates like a guiding star. You set your course and move in the direction you wish to go. As you move toward that goal, you attract and gather everything your goal requires to fulfill it.

When we reach our goal, we call ourselves successful. And we expect our lives to reflect that success.

Blair defines success as "the intentional, premeditated use of choice and decision" to attain what you desire. "Unless you choose – with certainty – what it is you want, you accept table scraps by default!"

It's not true that a big idea necessarily requires money. It does take thought and focus, which require discipline and action. The founder of Facebook, Mark Zuckerberg, started with an idea. He was in college and had no money, but he had a good idea that developed into a great one and took off. Money was always there at all the strategic moments. Now everyone in the world has heard about Facebook. Zuckerberg, while still in his twenties, became the youngest billionaire in the world.

Some people, like my mother, say they never had the opportunity to be a success. My mother, though she didn't believe it, actually was a success. She succeeded as a mother. She knew how to nurture and encourage her children. Each one of my siblings turned out to be a kind, upstanding citizen, contributing a little something to the world. But my mother's desire was to be a writer. She read a lot. But she allowed reading to take the place of writing. Nevertheless, at one point she started writing a novel. One day I spotted it lying on the dresser where we three girls combed our hair. I, too, was a big reader, but reading material was scarce. Here was something just begging to be read. As a young and curious child of ten, I picked it up and read it in my room. She caught me, grabbed it and put it back in its hiding place. Years later I asked her what happened to it and she confessed that she had finished it and then had burned it. She had no confidence in herself and her talents.

BEFORE PLANTING

The first thing we need to know before we can plant those seeds to grow success is precisely what we're on fire to do. We must be aware of our talent and how we'd like to express it. Don't you think that when you have a passion for something – even something that seems impractical or impossible – it might be your unique gift or talent calling out to you to express?

In most of us, our desire is just a seed. Nothing happens until we plant it. Seeds don't reveal what they can be until they are planted and nurtured and go through the development process.

A number of years ago, it was reported that some seeds were found in the pyramids, seeds that had been buried along with an ancient pharaoh. Those seeds had been scattered near his sarcophagus and lay there on the ground for thousands of years. A man who witnessed the tomb being unsealed picked up the seeds, took them home and planted them in his garden. They sprouted and flourished and produced wheat that ripened into gold. After thousands of years someone planted those seeds, so they realized their hidden potential.

Our potential is like seed. We have to make a decision what to plant. We have to choose to plant the seed. Then we have to commit ourselves to watering and tending that seed until it becomes more than a possibility. We cultivate it until it reaches maturity and gives up the fruits it has to offer.

Since talent is only potential, most of us have to develop it through constant practice. Few full-blown geniuses like Mozart are born. To practice our art, we have to develop our skills and master them. To do that can take thousands of hours. It means we have to stick with it until we develop it as completely as we can.

In my mother's case, she was intimidated by her lack of language skills. But if she'd had a true passion for writing, she would have used some of that reading time to study grammar and develop her vocabulary as well as her ability to use those tools and skills. But she never set a goal for herself. Maybe she didn't know it was important to do that. Even if we are gifted geniuses, if we don't set an objective, our genius may never find an outlet and we will always feel dissatisfied.

RIGHT GOALS

The objective, Gary Blair says, "is to choose the right goals, and then to create the necessary causes – the effects will follow."

The key words are "right goals" and "necessary causes."

First, let's examine goals. Some of us are afraid to set right goals that use our talents. We're not afraid to use goals to achieve small things. But we're afraid to set big goals. Why is that? We believe we're not good enough or powerful enough. We say, "Who am I to have big ideas?" Can't you just hear your parents scoff, "Who do you think you are?" Then you tell yourself, "I'm nobody. I don't have any power. My talent isn't that unique or important. What does the world need with what I have to offer?"

Setting right goals also means setting appropriate goals. If you long to be a great singer, you must first have a voice that can be trained. If you wish to write, you must write and develop your skill. You can't be a great singer if you have no voice, or a writer if you have no ability to express yourself on paper. This means examining yourself to determine if you have the potential to reach your goal, provided you do the work.

Next, let's examine necessary causes: you are cause to your goals because you are an integral part of the Universe. You are endowed with all of Its power and you set your idea into motion by deciding to experience that objective. There is, in reality, nothing you can't do – provided you have the talent and are willing to do what it takes.

The thing that can make us happy or scare us half to death, though, is the fact that the moment we commit to a big goal, we have sown seeds. We have turned them loose. And they are already starting the creative process. If you are too frightened to continue, you can always turn your back on those seeds, neglect them and let them die. But if you're committed to your goal and determined to achieve it, there's no backing out.

Your goal is now the guiding star. Your objective now compels you to make decisions every step of the way and keep on making decisions. It will bring people into your life that you never expected to meet. It will open doors you never expected to enter. Your life will change completely. We intuitively know that. That's why we may hesitate to set big goals. It means we'll have to move off the old crowded, beaten path and blaze a new one.

Every choice we make, now that we've set our goal, will be momentous. We are taking charge of our lives and creating a new "destiny." We are in reality changing the world, because what we do also matters to the world. Every move we make, every tiny change we make in our lives, does something to change the entire world. Believing you matter and what you do matters should be the impetuses to get you out of bed in the morning ready to do something to move your goal along.

Are you ready to set your new goal? Is it a big one? Is it a lifelong dream?

What if your goal today is to create a new business? You have an idea that will help people, bring some good into their lives and yours and even help make the world a better place. But you don't know how or where to start. You're frightened by the bigness of your idea. A frightened person might speculate, "What if I were to start a business, borrow a lot of money to stock my product and nobody bought it? Will it wind up just being wasted effort and money and time all over again? What if someone did buy my product and then bad-mouthed it to other people and my business goes down the tubes? Ah, I just won't do it. I'm kidding myself that I could succeed."

This is how that goal never gets realized. You allowed fear to talk you out of it.

Ernest Holmes, author of *The Science of Mind*, said that a successful person never thinks about failure. They never talk failure. They think and talk only success. That's good advice. People will tell you otherwise. They'll say you have to be realistic. Statistics say that ninety-five percent of new businesses fail within five years, most of them sooner.

Success occurs when you have set a goal and reached it. It doesn't matter how many times you have failed before you reach your goal. What matters is that you pick yourself up every time you fail and keep trying.

Success is doing it better and better until what you do is excellent. Improve your product or develop that skill or talent until it works for you, until you are proud of it and stand behind it one hundred percent. Every decision you make every day about your goal matters. Every tiny change or improvement you make in your plan matters. It's like the Butterfly Effect theory: tiny changes made all along the way can have enormous effects on the outcome.

Physicists say that when you change the way you look at something, the thing you look at changes in response.

The Science of Mind teaches us that we are cause to all the effects in our lives. We set things into motion. Success is built from the inside out.

What does this mean? It means we cannot set goals and then expect *not* to reach them. What's the point of deciding to achieve something unless you expect to achieve it? What you expect is very likely to happen. Your intention to achieve your goal causes the Universe to respond to you.

Yes, the Universe — all of it — responds to our intentions!

If you'd rather be scientific, we can call the Universe the Zero Field. That's what physicists call it now. They once claimed that an atom was the ultimate matter particle. Then they discovered that an atom isn't the ultimate particle. Below the atom lies the subatomic world of smaller and smaller particles. Then they discovered that below the subatomic particles is nothing but energy and information and — infinite possibility. This area is called the Zero Field, the Divine Matrix or the womb of the Universe, where all things begin.

Scientists are also calling the Zero Field *consciousness*. That's what we call it: consciousness. This is what is affected and goes to work for us the moment we decide on an idea and commit ourselves to it. Thoughts and ideas are the seeds of the physical world. All things begin with an idea. Your thoughts matter. Your feelings about your goals matter. Your expectations matter. Your thoughts are the seeds. Your feelings are the energy that powers them. Your expectations put you in alignment with the creative nature of the Universe.

Even more important, every thought has a frequency. You can measure a frequency. High energy, positive thoughts have a higher frequency than negative thoughts. That means that positive thoughts potentially create faster than negative ones.

John Assaraf, in his book *The Answer*, says, "Every thought you form broadcasts a distinct and particular frequency and that frequency elicits a response from the universe just as a hammer has an impact on the surface it strikes."

This means that success is not luck, nor is it accidental. Everything happens because of your choices. You are a part of the Universe. You use the same power. That means you have the ability and the power to cause your goals to happen. Your success begins and ends with you.

Let's say you've failed to achieve your goal several times. Analyze why that happened. And don't repeat the usual excuses: too much competition, not enough money, not enough time, the wrong time, in the wrong location, offering the wrong thing. These things matter, but they are not as important as the consciousness you did or did not develop during the process of going for your goal.

Ask yourself these questions:

Did I start out expecting to succeed,
or did I really expect to fail?

Did I have a vision? Was my vision clear?

What was my attitude all along the way?

Did I support my vision by keeping it at the forefront of my
mind and by being passionate about it?

Did I affirm daily that I was succeeding?

Did I encourage myself even when things looked bad,
or did I back off when I hit blocks, like competition
and lack of money?

Did I let doubt, fear or criticism keep me from learning
something I needed to know or doing what I needed to do?

Did I always do the best I could do?

Only we can determine what our best is. But if we decide
we're no good even before we've tried any new idea that comes
to us, we haven't given ourselves a fair shake.

Tony Robbins said, "...if you're not getting right results
from the questions you ask yourself, then ask a better question."
When setting your goal, ask yourself:

What does my goal look and feel like?

How do I expect my life to change when
I've achieved my goal?

What is my future life like when I am a success?

Is this goal something I'm passionate about and wish to live
with and explore for years to come?

Define your goal in more and greater detail. The end result
you start with is only the idea. It must become more real to you
every day, so real you can see it, feel it, taste it, almost touch it.

What if your goal were to write a book? Maybe you've already
tried to write a book. At least you finished it. But after several of
your friends read it, they told you it was awful. And no agent would
represent it. Should you give up on the idea of being an author?

In this example, you would ask yourself:

Am I really a writer?

Do I have a writer's skills?

Can I express myself well in prose form,
in a screenplay or poetry?

Am I truly passionate about writing?

Do I really like spending all that time alone?

If the answers to these questions are yes, then set a specific goal, such as writing a specific book. Use affirmations like these:

I WRITE AN EXCELLENT BOOK THAT IS NOT ONLY PUBLISHED BUT IS ALSO SO PROVOCATIVE THAT IT'S A BEST-SELLER.

I SEE MYSELF TRAVELING ALL OVER THE COUNTRY SPEAKING TO CROWDS IN BOOKSTORES, DOING READINGS, AUTOGRAPHING THOUSANDS OF MY BOOKS.

MY BOOKS EARN MILLIONS OF DOLLARS.

I AM INTERVIEWED ON HUNDREDS OF TV SHOWS ABOUT MY BOOK.

I GET A MILLION-DOLLAR ADVANCE ON MY NEXT BOOK.

Thinking and affirming like this develops the consciousness of your goal. Because, you see, the quality of the ideas you put in to develop your goal determines the quality you will take out.

It's up to you to define what success looks like for you. Set and develop the best possible goals for yourself. Even if they seem unattainable, if you believe in them enough to do what is necessary, you can succeed – again, if you do what it takes.

As Blair said, "Goals are the seeds. You become only what you plant. The quality of the harvest is a direct result of the quality of your seeds and your decisions."

Being decisive is important. Keeping yourself committed to your goal is just as important. Commitment will help you recognize and take advantage of opportunities to develop your skills and talents even further. Commitment will help you to be the best you can be at what you've undertaken.

Then step out into the unknown. The known is where you are. It's where you've been and it is what's holding you back.

If you're ever going to change where you are, you have to do the thing you've never done before, go where you've never gone before and be more uncomfortable than you've ever been before. And this means developing your consciousness so that you are prepared to receive the fruits of the seeds you have planted.

RECEIVING SUCCESS

We've carefully chosen our goals, planted the seeds, developed our consciousness, kept our vision of success in place and BAM! All of a sudden, our goal is right in front of us, faster than we expected. But soon it begins to crumble and fall apart – one more time! What is going on here?

It may fall apart because we have not embodied our idea completely in consciousness. Consciousness is the ground where the seed has been sowed. And each seed requires a certain amount of time to mature. Bamboo, for instance, can take three years to become deeply rooted. Not a sprig breaks through the ground for those three years. An ignorant planter might give up, but the wise planter understands that once the bamboo erupts, it shoots a hundred feet into the air in the first year of its growth.

So it may be that in our enthusiasm to see our idea fulfilled, we override the requirements to fully embody the idea. If we don't have it solidly embodied, we may not be able to hold on to it. That's when it looks like we might have failed – one more time.

To succeed solidly, set your goal. Commit to it. Sow your seeds. Nurture them. Don't be in a hurry. There's an old truism: "He who hurries does not trust." In other words, if we're in a hurry, there's a subtle belief that if we don't hurry up, it won't be there for us or it will melt into thin air. What it means is take the time to do all the work necessary, learn what you need to learn, make sure your skills match what is necessary to achieve your goal. Then, when you reach your goal you will be ready for it in every way possible.

Ernest Holmes illustrated that work with an affirmation:

TODAY THE POSSIBILITIES OF MY EXPERIENCE ARE
UNLIMITED. THE SPIRIT FLOWS THROUGH ME, INSPIRING
ME AND SUSTAINING THAT INSPIRATION. I HAVE ABILITY
AND TALENT AND I AM BUSY USING THEM. THIS TALENT IS
DIVINELY SUSTAINED AND MARKETED UNDER A UNIVERSAL
PLAN OF RIGHT ACTION.

Ernest also said, "We may assume that spiritual man is
already a success, is already supplied with everything he needs.
The potential of all things exists in the Universal Wholeness."

You are whole and complete right now. That wholeness
will forever include your success. All the work you need to do
is simply express it. That's simply how life works...

...the Science of Mind way.

CHAPTER 2

Beyond Wealth

How to Create Prosperity

———•◦•———

Which is normal, prosperity or poverty? The answer is: prosperity. Poverty is abnormal.

What causes prosperity? What causes poverty? There is only one answer for both questions. They are created by what you believe and how you think.

Poverty is abnormal. Prosperity is normal. You might dispute that from what you read and from your personal experience. It does seem as if most of the world is poor. Don't you get those emails telling you that if you have shoes and clothes and sleep indoors and have three regular meals a day, that you are better off than ninety-five percent of the world? I do. Those emails have their purpose. They help us to remember to be grateful and not to forget those people who don't have very much.

Most of the world believes that poverty is the normal fact of life. Why do they believe that? Because they truly believe that our resources are limited. No matter what we believe, the truth is that our resources are unlimited. Distribution methods, they say, are the only limitation. And that, too, is perhaps a belief.

What most of the world doesn't know is that everyone lives by spiritual laws. Most people scratch their heads and look puzzled if you mention spiritual laws. What do you mean by spiritual laws, they ask?

SPIRITUAL LAWS

Spiritual laws are the unseen forces by which the Universe operates. There are Universal principles or creative laws that everyone uses every time they think. Even if you're not aware of them, you're still using them. And because you're unaware, you might not be using them for your greater benefit. You may even be using them to your detriment if you are accustomed to judging by the appearances around you. All of us have the tendency to believe more in what we see and hear than in what we can't see: those invisible laws.

If you don't know how life works, you may believe that you were born to poverty and that it will be nearly impossible for you ever to become prosperous. You will live your life without a sense of purpose. You may never set any goals for yourself and never expect to get any satisfaction out of living.

These life principles I'm talking about have been known for centuries, even thousands of years. But as they reported in *The Secret*, perhaps people who knew about these laws did their best to keep them hidden from the world at large. If you don't know how life works, then you are working in the dark. You are dependent on "people who know." You can be controlled, used and manipulated by fear and superstition, by religion and threats of punishment. And, of course, history reveals to us that the majority of people have been used to serve the purposes of a few.

To understand the Creative Life Principle is to liberate yourself from fear, superstition and manipulation. How is this so? If you are aware that you were born with this principle — that you came here with it as a part of your nature — then this Truth will set you free to use these laws to serve your own highest good.

The Creative Life Principle will serve your highest good. Why? Because its nature is goodness. When we use it according to its nature, it will create good in our lives. If we are aware of It, It serves us. If we are not aware of It, It can enslave us. Intelligence, life, abundance, order, harmony, satisfaction, fulfillment, health, love, joy and beauty are its nature. If you use these very powerful laws to hurt, injure or kill, they rebound and bring the same thing back to you. And the result will appear to be punishment.

Physicists tell us that there is only one Power and one Substance that all of us use. There is just Intelligent Energy that we think into and It takes on the form and nature of our thoughts.

Prosperity, then, is a way of thinking into that Intelligent Energy. Poverty is also a way of thinking into that Intelligent Energy. But if we're aware that our thinking is using a creative principle, we can increase our consciousness of wealth and manifest abundance.

Do you consider yourself a prosperous person? Maybe you do. But maybe you'd also like to have a little more than you have. My family always believed they'd get by. And we always did. My husband promised me that we'd always have enough. And we always have had enough. But I thought we should have more than enough. Didn't Mae West say, "Too much of a good thing is wonderful!"?

What does prosperity mean to you at the fundamental level?

My definition of prosperity means that we are at peace within ourselves and that we are free to do whatever we'd like to do, whenever we wish to do it.

I grew up in a family of limited means. By that, I mean that we didn't have a lot of money. My father was a laborer in a brick plant; my mother worked in a sewing factory. Both worked very hard for the little wages they earned. Today, as I look back and measure our lives by my definition of prosperity, I realize that my family was, in fact, quite prosperous. Yes, they worked hard. Yes, we didn't have a lot of money. But if any of us wished to have something, sooner or later we had it. We didn't go into debt for anything. We saved up and bought it, from bicycles to appliances.

Our imaginations might have been rather limited, I think. We didn't wish for huge things. However, I had lots of pretty clothes that my mother made for me. I always had some coins for treats after school. I had all the school supplies I needed. I was never denied anything necessary, and I even had a few unnecessary luxuries.

In school I won awards and trips that kept life interesting. I also nurtured a grand ambition and kept my eye on my goal until I attained it. I was already living by the Creative Life Principle, but I wasn't aware that I was.

As most people do, my mother used this law without being aware she was doing so. When obstacles came between her and what she thought was necessary or right, she made daring and authoritative declarations. I remember the year my sister was making plans to enroll in college. She had made up her mind to go only just weeks before the term began. She and my mother went over to the college to register and to inquire about a loan. They were too late, the dean of women told them. The supply of money available for lending was exhausted. They were out of luck.

My sister was crushed. So was my mother. They left the office, walked out and sat on a wall just outside the campus. Both were depressed. My sister began to sob and covered her tears with her sunglasses. My mother heard her sobs and told her, "Don't you cry! You're going to college. You're going to this one. We'll find a way!"

The words were no sooner out of her mouth than down the walk toward them hurried the dean of women. "Oh, there you are!" she called. "I was afraid you'd already left. I found some money for you!" My sister got her loan and she went to college. She became a teacher and paid back that loan.

The word, declared with authority and conviction, set aside any conditions of limitation and revealed what they needed. They needed a loan. That's prosperity. It's having the right things appear at the right time.

PROSPERITY

I've read many books about creating money, wealth and prosperity. They all pretty much say the same thing, just in different words.

Prosperity is not just money. Money is only one aspect. Prosperity is a spiritual idea; it is love in action. Love is giving. Giving is the major, creative activity of Spirit. That's what Spirit does; it creates by giving Itself and becoming what It creates. There is no limitation in Spirit. It can't know something unlike Itself. Its nature is to create, to give and to express.

Prosperity is living without limitation. Prosperity is an active thing. Perhaps you are already aware of the economic theory of supply and demand. In Science of Mind, it's demand and supply. We make our claim on the Creative Life Principle, build a consciousness of what we'd like to experience and voila! Supply arrives.

Let's take some time to get a better understanding of prosperity and how to create it. There are four primary factors for creating prosperity.

FOUR FACTORS TO CREATE PROSPERITY

1. Visualize prosperity and what it means to you. My personal definition of prosperity is being at peace with myself and being free to do whatever I'd like to do whenever I wish to do it.

2. Clearly define your goal and know where you'd like to go if you're going to achieve it.

3. Know yourself and how you're going to proceed. That means looking at yourself to see if you have the talent and skills you need to achieve your goal.

4. Take action. Even if you have the skills, talent and capabilities necessary to achieve the goals that you are trained to achieve, if you don't act on them, they remain a dream.

Once you're clear on these four factors, there are five essentials that will help you utilize the Creative Life Principle.

FIVE ESSENTIALS TO UTILIZE THE CREATIVE LIFE PRINCIPLE

1. Develop the confidence that you can create prosperity. Overcome your doubts about your own abilities and perhaps your feelings of unworthiness to be prosperous.

How do you go about that? By first knowing who you are. You individuate the One Life, the One Substance, the

One Infinite Intelligence and Wisdom, the One Power that some people call God. It is unlimited and everything comes from it. It can create anything anyone can imagine. Since you live within it, you are inseparable from it and derive your substance, intelligence and power from it. How could you be deficient or unworthy of any good? When you meditate on this, know this and believe it in your heart of hearts, you realize that it's simply not possible for you to be deficient or unworthy of any good.

Good awaits only your belief in it. You simply have to think about who you are and all the reasons I listed above explaining why you can have anything you are able to visualize. Develop your belief in this. Allow your belief to grow and mature in your consciousness.

You may at this moment doubt that you can have anything you want. And of course, you can't have anything you simply *want*. But you can have anything you believe you can have. If you wish to be prosperous, it is possible for you to be prosperous.

But it requires the underpinning of right thinking to support prosperity. That means you will be required all by yourself to do the mental work it takes to build the consciousness of prosperity.

To keep yourself from entertaining doubts, you may have to shut off the news, the reports of joblessness, of the recession and of the yo-yoing economy so you won't be influenced by the negativity. You will be influenced against your own best interests if you allow these negative reports to enter your mind space. Thoughts that oppose prosperity tend to neutralize all your spiritual work if you are not alert. It takes alertness and standing guard at the doorway of your mind, allowing nothing in that does not support your ideas of prosperity.

This is where the hard work begins and your determination will be tested. Not many people are born with a consciousness of prosperity. On the whole, it has to be developed. Yes, people are born into wealth. Their fathers or mothers made lots of money. But when children are handed their inheritance, very often they squander it. Why? Because they haven't earned the consciousness that fosters prosperity.

2.   Listen to the desires of your heart. There is something you came here to do, so do it. It may involve some risk. But no one ever lives fully unless he or she is doing what their heart tells them to do.

In an advice column that I read not long ago, a young man wrote that he had a secure, well-paying job but it didn't satisfy him. He asked if he should give it up and go out there in the cold and look for that thing that would satisfy him. The columnist advised him to stay put and pursue hobbies and activities that would awaken the passion in him. Perhaps the thing he was looking for would just appear at his door one day.

Just as the columnist wrote, I would never advise anyone to give up a job that supports them. At the same time, it is important to start working on the thing that gives you the greater satisfaction. It may take some self-examination to arrive at that knowledge. This young man might ask himself if he can live with less money to start with. Is security all that important at his young age? Does he have a clear goal in mind, and is he prepared to achieve it?

3. Cultivate the Creative Life Principle. Cultivate the conviction that you embody the unlimited power of the Creative Life Principle. You can learn about it in classes and talk about it with knowledge, but until you put it to the test more than once, you'll never have more than a surface conviction of it. To achieve real prosperity, you must be convinced that an impersonal but infinitely intelligent Law knows exactly how to bring your desires to fruition. You must not doubt but know that this Law is working for your highest good at all times.

4. Work in alignment with Spirit's nature. What does this mean? It means that Spirit's nature is creative. Since it is unlimited, all-powerful, all-knowing Intelligence and eternal, so are you. It is Life itself. It is goodness. It is peace, joy, harmony, beauty and love. Align yourself with the nature of Spirit daily and tell yourself that it is flowing through you.

Next, think, say and do the things that express constructively, that never degrade or impoverish another person (or yourself and for that matter). Ask yourself before you think it or do it:

Is it life-affirming for you and everyone?

Will it bless you and hurt no one?

Will it move you forward in life and satisfy you?

As you align with your higher nature, you will develop a constructive outlook on life. You will be balanced emotionally, not given to sudden highs and lows. You will make intelligent and wise decisions that move you forward. You will think more clearly. You will be living your prosperity actively. Why? Because once you are living in alignment with the Law of Prosperity, prosperity will be the result.

5. Be aware of how you are living. If you have aligned with spiritual qualities, your life should be improving. Things seem easier to accomplish. You meet the right people who are eager to help you. They may come into your life to do just one thing and leave as soon as they've done the job. You may find yourself receiving unexpected bonuses and awards. Everything gets better. It doesn't mean you won't have some ups and downs and even some setbacks. But look at every setback and downturn as a side trip to pick up some necessary element of your success.

Be aware of your thinking and with what qualities you're feeding your subconscious mind. Be very aware that it is the right ideas you are feeding the subconscious that is building your prosperity. The subconscious is the phase of mind that will make something out of your beliefs and daily thoughts. Because of this, it is vital that you watch what you are consciously thinking. You have to be more alert and alive than you ever were before.

DEALING WITH OLD THOUGHTS
OF UNWORTHINESS

As you move forward building your consciousness of prosperity, you may be confronted with many of the old fears and demons that you've lived with since childhood. We all have thoughts and beliefs of unworthiness, of not being good enough or talented enough. And as they come up they must be dealt with, neutralized or dissolved and released. They come up because they contradict your consciously created ideas of prosperity. So don't be surprised when they come. These are old habitual patterns and are in context with your old consciousness. Don't let them impress you. Don't struggle with them or get entangled with them. Release them and know they cannot distract or override your consciousness.

BUILDING A CONSCIOUSNESS OF PROSPERITY

You are now going to begin building a consciousness of prosperity. How are you going to do that? By conditioning your mind or consciousness through spiritual mind treatment (also known as affirmative prayer) and affirmations. When you pray, you are praying to your own consciousness. Why? Because that's where Spirit is. Within you. Within all of us. We don't pray to God, Spirit, First Cause, the Creator of all that is. We pray *as* God, because First Cause is within our consciousness. Our prayers simply affirm what is already possible, what already exists as potential in the invisible. Our prayers release the possible.

The Field of consciousness exists as a state of infinite possibility. There is no limit to what can be created from it, for all raw materials exist there. When we decide to experience something and focus on that idea and think into that field, infinite possibility folds down and becomes that one particular possibility.

In other words, you make a choice to focus on something – in this case building a consciousness of abundance. If you continue to focus on the idea of prosperity and continue to add more ideas to it, open your mind up to new ideas, the Creative Life Principle goes to work and builds that idea into a concrete experience or form. As long as you keep focusing on your idea, it will continue to grow in the invisible, and ultimately it will burst out as a matured and fully developed experience.

This means that your ideas, your thoughts and your beliefs are the seeds and roots of your experiences. When you think about anything, negative or positive, you are beginning to birth the thing to which you have been paying attention. Write this in your consciousness: What I think matters. What I think matters. What I think is acted upon by a Creative Law that is always listening to me and creates for me personally. Watch what you are paying attention to!

Now that we understand that what we think matters, make a conscious choice to think thoughts that become the building blocks of your experience of prosperity. Think prosperity thoughts. You know what they are – if you now know what prosperity looks like to you (you can discover this by working through this book's earlier exercises).

This means you must refuse to talk about how awful the economy is and how terribly everyone is suffering with less money and fewer jobs. Every time you find yourself thinking those thoughts, negate them. Press the delete button. Delete!

THOUGHT PATTERNS TO BUILD CONSCIOUSNESS

In the following five segments, let's consider thought patterns that will definitely build and support a consciousness of prosperity.

1. Meditate on abundance. Meditate on the idea that the Universe is weighted on the side of abundance. One seed can foster and grow a plant that produces hundreds of fruits and thousands of seeds. One seed eventually can feed the world.

The story goes that Sir Francis Drake, after battling the Spaniards in the Caribbean, stopped at Cartagena in Colombia to collect provisions; he picked up a few strange little tubers, later called potatoes. Next he stopped at Roanoke Island to rescue a small number of English settlers who had tried to start a colony there and failed. The settlers took the potatoes back to England and discovered how easy they were to grow. They were also easy to harvest, using only a spade. A few little tubers mushroomed into enough potatoes to feed a whole continent in just a few years.

Use your imagination and apply a little energy to get started. Imagination and energy are the only tools we need to produce abundant prosperity. Thinking constructively is vitally important because what we think multiplies rampantly, just as seeds do.

If you've been pessimistic lately, sit down and rethink those dour thoughts. Are you angry and resentful because you don't seem to be getting your share of the pie? If so, remember that everything tends to multiply, even anger and resentment. Look yourself square in the eye and tell yourself to shape up. Realign your thoughts with the nature of Spirit. Spirit can't be negative or blue or doubtful, resentful or jealous. It's not Spirit's nature to be anything but powerful and joyful. It can and will produce whatever it desires... through you, as you.

Know that no one is against you having prosperity, not even the economy. The Universe is for you. You have everything you need within your own mind to create abundance. The only enemy you will ever have is your own negative thinking, and your thoughts can be reversed to work for your highest good.

2. Spiritual leverage. In the business world, if you wish to build a big company, you need financial leverage. Well, you already have the right kind of leverage you need to build anything you desire. It's called spiritual leverage. The Creative Law is present and infinitely intelligent, as well as powerful. It will accept and work with any thought you give it and find the way to produce it for you. That's why it's good to ignore statistics, the status quo, and all the beliefs that tell you that you don't have a chance because you're a small fish in an ocean of sharks. Every single day, acknowledge that the Universe is leveraged in your favor. All the power is already on your side. Your faith in your spiritual power can move mountains.

3. Overflowing gratefulness. You've heard it said so often that it's become a New Thought cliché: *Cultivate an attitude of gratitude.* You know it and you may even say it, but do you actually practice gratitude other than on Thanksgiving? Are you really grateful for what you already have, or do you grudgingly take what good you have for granted? Do you really appreciate your life, your health, the money you have and the people in your life who stay around, no matter how cranky you are? Do you really feel gratitude that you are meeting your bills and that you have enough of everything today? You say you do, but if you really feel gratitude, you'll get a lift of joy in your chest every time you express it sincerely.

If you don't feel gratitude, you will not only be unable to accept more prosperity but you'll also have a hard time accepting people and conditions as they are. You may resort to criticism instead. Perhaps you've concluded that no one is as good as they ought to be. Nothing ever turns out the way you think it should. Criticism is a form of hatred and the worst kind of ingratitude. This is not an attitude that promotes abundance. In fact, it promotes smallness and loneliness. It keeps people and things away from you. It diminishes you and the quality of your life.

How can you do it better? You can choose to let go of the negative judgments just as soon as they cross your mind. Ask yourself, who is this person I'm criticizing? Am I better or lower than this person? The answer is no, I am one with this person. We are one with the One. No one is better and no one is less than I. I refuse to allow criticism and rejection to cross my mind a single moment longer. I don't have to be friends with someone with whom I have nothing in common, but I don't have to savage them to keep them away.

Accept everyone for who they are: an individualization of Spirit. This doesn't mean you accept their bad behavior; you accept them and who they are. Acceptance clears the way to receive. To receive more, it's necessary to stay open and receptive, both giving and receiving. It's a two-lane street. You have to use both lanes and keep them open both ways for abundance to arrive and for it to circulate and move out again.

Make a habit of giving away some of what you have. If you have no money to give, give service. Give it without expecting anything in return. Give for the pure joy of giving. I know people who do great service and when they talk about it they are radiant with the light of love. I love hearing them talk about it because I get spillover from it and feel good as well. To do things for people for the pure joy of it is part of my feeling prosperous. Everyone is enriched when they give freely.

Giving for the pure joy of giving is in perfect alignment with the nature of Spirit, Love, Joy.

"Gratitude is an affirmation that life is presenting you with another gift from its infinite cache of riches," wrote one sage. "Gratitude is seeing good right where you are and working with it."

4. Infinite mind. Be open to new ideas. William Blake wrote: "The man who never alters his opinions is like standing water, and breeds reptiles of the mind." We stagnate when we don't open ourselves to fresh ideas. Like a pond that has no outlet, it breeds all kinds of fungi, algae and icky things. Fresh water has to flow in constantly if the pond is to remain healthy.

If you aren't open to new ideas, you'll be stuck with your old stale ideas that perpetuate the status quo: believing that you never have enough. Without new ideas you may never have enough. And what you have may be lost, deteriorate or diminish.

Why aren't people open to new ideas? Because they are afraid new ideas might be disturbing. New ideas sometimes compel people to make changes in their lives. They may feel compelled to take some action. When changes occur, things get chaotic, like anything under construction. New ideas may upset you for a while. You may stay shaky for a while, but again, make a conscious choice to open yourself to new ideas, new information and even new training.

Decide to say "yes" to the new. Say "yes" to ideas that stimulate you and shake you to your core. Examine them and see how they might work for you. After all, they have appeared because you've asked for them. Undoubtedly they bring something to prosper you. New ideas keep you alive and healthy. New ideas keep you excited about life and keep you expecting surprises and delights. Paraphrasing Yogi Berra: "You aren't dead until you're dead." Live till the last day. Live and say "yes" to the new. Know that because you think from the Infinite Mind, all of its wisdom and intelligence are available to you to use to create anything you can focus on.

5. Respectfulness. Examine the Golden Rule and begin to live by it as often as you can. Anyone can do this. It is the law of cause and effect. Most of us are insulted and hurt when people treat us disrespectfully. "How dare they?" we cry.

I've found that when people insult me or treat me badly, I've usually started it either thoughtlessly or deliberately. If I talk to someone before I've resolved anger or hurt or a momentary loss of self-esteem, I will invariably offend someone. I won't be as considerate and kind as I'd like them to be to me. I often have to stop and ask myself, "What would I like to have happen here?" And then I try to think like that, act like that and be like that.

Again, living by the Golden Rule means we have to think, speak and live with awareness.

Be very conscious of what you're putting out there for people to react to. Choose to treat people as you wish to be treated. Wouldn't you like to wake up the whole world to the truth that each person is responsible for the condition of his or her personal relationships, as well as for our relationships nationally and internationally? Everyone will eventually get back what he or she has put out into the Universe.

As Ralph Waldo Emerson said, "If you need a friend, first be a friend." Do you wish for people to love you? Then love them first. How do you love people you don't know? Love them by knowing who they are. This is the highest degree of love: understanding who people are and treating them with the reverence and respect they deserve.

You can't mouth the word "love" and then treat people as if they were unimportant. Are you treating every person you meet with reverence – because you know who everyone is? Do you respect their rights along with your own?

The Golden Rule is: As you sow, so shall you reap. Gandhi said, "I must first be what I wish to see in the world." If you wish to be at peace with yourself, then you must live it and be it. To be at peace and to have good in mind equally for everyone else puts you in perfect alignment with the Law of Prosperity. Good relationships, respect and love will be the demonstration.

BREAKING OLD PATTERNS

If you are already at work applying the ideas you learned in earlier chapters, you've already defined what prosperity means to you, what it looks like and how it feels. Maybe you're feeling a bit frustrated because you wish it would happen sooner.

Have you ever had the experience of making affirmation after affirmation and nothing happened? I have. It happened in the early days of studying Science of Mind. I wondered what I was doing wrong. I asked myself, "What in my thought is causing nothing to happen?" Ask a question; get an answer. It was illustrated very clearly for me. My attention was immediately drawn to some people close to me and their attitude about money.

This was before I had defined my idea of prosperity as being at peace with myself, and being free to do whatever I would'd liked, whenever I wished to do it. I used to have a negative attitude about money. It was so subtle that I was hardly aware of it. No doubt I'd inherited it from my extended family.

Even though we didn't have much money, my family eventually seemed to acquire whatever we needed, and even had a few luxuries. But aunts and uncles and cousins who visited us frequently had some pretty negative ideas about people who had money. One of my earliest memories was a cousin saying, "People with money are stuck up. They have swelled heads. They are snobs." People, in my cousin's belief, had to earn their money. It was doubtful that the rich had ever earned their money. This cousin in particular made it clear that she believed rich people were basically immoral people.

Though I agreed out loud with her, secretly I didn't believe that. Why not? Well, I strongly desired to be rich too. And what was wrong with being rich? Rich people had it easy. They drove nice cars. They wore nice clothes. They looked better than we did. They never got dirty. They went to Florida in the winter and came back with suntans. Who wouldn't want to do that?

One day, I heard someone I loved very much sneer at a rich woman she knew only in passing. She repeated what we'd heard that cousin say: "She thinks she's something because she has money. She's such a snob." I knew this relative was struggling to pay bills and would have loved to have more money. She was working metaphysically to demonstrate money to pay off her bills. But she put down people who had money.

I, too, was doing my spiritual work daily to demonstrate more money, and it struck me that I had those thoughts too, but they were hiding way down deep in my subconscious and rarely surfaced. But they were there. And they did surface when called upon by others. It dawned on me that I too might be working against my own good by holding onto these belief patterns.

I asked this person, "If you believe money is basically bad, why do you want it?" She wanted to be a good person, she said. But she also wished to be financially free. It dawned on me then and there that she might be neutralizing her own work. At the same time, I knew that I too needed to do some internal house cleaning if I were going to have more.

You see, the mind that's listening to your words and gauging your feelings believes every word you say. The Creative Law of mind hears what you say and believe about other people. It thinks that the words you speak are what you desire for yourself. That's why it's important to be clear about the message you are sending to the Creative Law.

Another important thing to remember is that the Creative Law can't act if you give it conflicting instructions. On the one hand, maybe you've begun to declare and affirm that you have money to burn. But the thought comes up that "People with money are bad people." Those ideas are in conflict. One affirmation says "yes," the other says "no." You are neutralizing your positive affirmations with your negative affirmations and beliefs about others.

The law picks up on, works with and manifests your dominant thoughts and feelings. When you have clear, strong thoughts and feelings that are constructive, there is no conflict. The law must and will act.

When you (consciously or subconsciously) declare negative things about people with money, you're actually envying them. You don't have money and you know you are a good person. They have it and therefore they must be bad people. But you, too, need money to live on, to buy food and pay your bills. And maybe you'd also like a sixty-two inch HDTV connected to DirecTV with HBO and Showtime. Envy is a strong message you're sending to your subconscious mind. Envy says, "I don't have, I don't have." Envy is a strong feeling. Strong feelings set the law into motion. With envy, the Law recognizes "I don't have, I don't have" and sends back not having. The Law is working fine. But it's producing "I don't have" in your life.

The one who is not working fine is you – or I. When we're jealous or envious or angry, we're setting the law into motion to create a void in our lives. And when that happens, of course, we will feel anything but prosperous.

In the Book of James in the New Testament, we read, "A double-minded man is unstable in all his ways." A wise saying, because you can't get anywhere or move from where you are if you take one step forward and then one step back. You have to choose the direction toward which you are going to go, in thought, in word and in deed. By not choosing to continue affirming, "I HAVE ALL THE MONEY I NEED," you don't become prosperous. You have to decide to take a stand, break the habit of saying one thing but believing another.

How do you break the habit of envy and jealousy? Start by being grateful for what the other person has. I know, that sounds difficult. It hurts to see someone enjoying just what you'd like to have. But they didn't take it away from you. They demonstrated it by creating it in consciousness. Every person on this planet has what he or she has because of what they truly believe in their heart of hearts. You can't fool the law. It will produce from your dearest held beliefs.

Give thanks, then, for others people's good. Then give thanks for what you have. Every time you are tempted to feel envy or jealousy, give thanks for some good in your life. If the only good thing you can think of is that you're alive, then give thanks that you are alive today.

In the previous chapter, I wrote about how to build five thought patterns to produce prosperity. If you are questioning why you have to do that or why you have to clean up the way you think in order to manifest prosperity, here's the reason why: The way you think will either help you move forward into prosperity, neutralize any move toward it or actually move you backward.

All creation begins with an idea or thought. The technology that has moved us forward so rapidly the last few years certainly began with ideas. All of our experiences begin, first, with an idea.

If you wish to be prosperous, you need to begin to think the thoughts that produce it.

THOUGHT PATTERNS THAT PRODUCE PROSPERITY

Let's review the first five thought patterns described previously:

1. Meditate on the idea that the nature of the Universe is abundance. See abundance everywhere and claim it for yourself.

2. Realize that you have Spiritual Leverage working for you. Why? You individualize Spirit and embody all Its power. All of it is working for you. That's leverage and then some!

3. Allow your gratefulness to overflow. We can't be grateful if we are filling our minds with not having and despising those who do have.

4. Be open to new ideas with an Infinite Mind. You can't resist new ideas and move ahead. If you wish to change the status quo, you have to welcome new ideas that will create more for you.

5. Be respectful of others by applying the Golden Rule. It is the law of cause and effect. What you put out with your words, feelings and actions will return to you.

All of these are easy to do, but most of us don't do them with any consistency. Once we consistently apply these ideas, prosperity is inevitable.

Let's continue building new thought patterns and neutralizing the old patterns of thinking.

6. Understand the true nature of your intuitive goodness. The questions I get most often are, "If there is no God who rewards and punishes, why then do I have to be a good person? Why can't I take my good by any method I choose? So what if I deprive other people? If I don't take my share I might be left out. If there's no God, then it's every man for himself."

That's the kind of thinking that deprives you of prosperity.

Science of Mind teaches that every single one of us individualizes goodness, and that we intuitively wish to express our true nature. We also intuitively know that we are one with everyone, that they are the same at essence as we are. All people everywhere are one with us. When we take from or hurt someone else, we hurt ourselves.

What you put out rebounds to you. There's a perfect safeguard written into the law of cause and effect. The Law, if you recall, responds to everything you think, say and believe. It responds by creating an experience for you. That's why your hatred for someone else only does something negative to you. The result may seem like a punishment. That's also why when you love someone, you get a loving response back. That may seem like a reward. But you are giving only to yourself, whether you love or hate.

I used to hear my grandma mutter darkly, "What goes around comes around. She'll get hers!" It sounded like something horrible to me, and as a result I didn't want to believe in the law.

Send only the things you are sure you'd wish to return lavishly. You definitely know what those things are. There will be no confusion about that. Simple, isn't it?

7. Become aware of the intelligence you were born to express. Wake up and become aware that you are programmed from the day you arrived on earth until this present day.

All of us are endowed with intelligence, but we have to learn how to use it. We learn how to use it by thinking. But much of what we think is not our own; it is given to us by our families, our teachers, the politicians and the media. It's a never-ending process. Our experience generally reflects what we listen to and absorb.

Our religious beliefs are the same; they have been fed to us by our parents and by our churches. Some of us learned our catechism at Catholic school. Some of us listened to preachers on Sunday. We simply accepted what they said as honest truth – until we began to sort through and think about the ideas we'd learned.

We can just as easily accept the ideas of Science of Mind and use them. But it's always a good idea to think through any new idea. Through what Science of Mind teaches about our identity, we can actively begin to know ourselves and make better decisions.

When you know you are free to choose the better and are not subject to destiny, you can, in very little time, break through the programming of a lifetime. You have to do this yourself, though, and with enough hard work and dedication it will eventually feel normal to you.

8. Put your thoughts into action. A quick way to neutralize old poverty thoughts and break through a pattern of lack is to act and believe that you're already prosperous.

Edwene Gaines was dirt poor when she began to study metaphysics. She was told to act as if she were rich and she would become so. At one point, she and a friend decided they'd like to vacation in Mexico. Edwene had no money at all for the trip and didn't know where or how she could get any. So she decided to demonstrate the trip through treatment. She started making affirmation after affirmation, but nothing turned up.

She soon grew frustrated. She gradually caught on to the fact that she wasn't going to have a demonstration just by thinking and saying words over and over.

She went to her metaphysical teacher and asked her what else she could do to speed her demonstration. Her teacher told her that she wasn't going to manifest riches until she *felt* rich. She had to find a way to feel rich. Her teacher suggested that she go out and buy something for herself – at the level she could afford – that would make her feel rich.

Edwene had always loved olives stuffed with almonds. They were a luxury because they were more expensive than plain olives, so she didn't buy them. Just spending the extra money for almond-stuffed olives put a hole in her very modest budget.

But because she felt rich when she ate them, she decided to go out and buy them. At the market, she casually picked up a bottle and dropped it into her shopping cart. As she looked down at them, they twinkled as if they were solid gold. She was sure that rich people ate only almond-stuffed olives. She called her girlfriend to come over and bring a bottle of wine, her new crystal wine glasses and a crystal bowl for the olives. They sat by the pool, ate the olives and drank the wine and pretended they were already in Mexico. Edwene said she felt rich, really rich.

She had done everything she had learned to do, but still nothing happened. The day was approaching when she needed to pay for the tickets if she were going to go to Mexico. She started to drive to the travel agent, but on a hunch, sidetracked and drove over to her mother's house instead. At the foot of the long driveway, she stopped to pick up the mail in the mailbox and was surprised to find a letter addressed to her. It was from a former roommate. The letter contained a check for Edwene for her share of the furniture her roommate had recently sold. The amount of the check was exactly the amount she needed to buy her ticket to Mexico.

We love to hear these stories, but we forget that it could happen to us as well. We, too, can demonstrate even greater things if we keep our mind fixed on our goal and make sure that most of our thoughts and feelings foster its growth.

9. Have the courage and confidence that you will manifest your idea of prosperity. Faith and trust will enable you to stand firm with your declarations and affirmations in the face of everything that denies your good.

A year or so ago, a client called me, desperate for help. Her rent was due the next day and she didn't have a dollar. I took a firm stand for her. I told her it was guaranteed that she would have her rent by tomorrow, provided she didn't back off and quiver in fear and speculate on what would happen if she didn't have it. The result was that ten minutes later, an aunt called to tell her she was sending her a check. The amount of the check was more than enough to pay the rent.

Courage can be learned. Edwene learned to be courageous. She didn't give up when no money appeared to pay for her plane ticket. She continued to do the necessary work and when that didn't seem effective, she asked her teacher for further enlightenment. She continued to develop the feeling that she was rich. She persisted with enthusiasm and expectation.

Most of us give up too soon. The Universe sent me a note on Wednesday. It read, "For the one who continues, failure becomes impossible. Phew! The Universe."

It came at just the right time for me, because I had been tempted to give up on a goal I had been treating for. I re-established my belief in it and have decided to continue in the face of all kinds of old thought patterns that rise and speak to me of failure. I choose to persist. I choose to speak the truth and stand for what I wish to do in the face of everything that denies my goals.

You must develop the courage to keep your consciousness elevated in the Absolute, where anything is possible. Continue to expect to reach your goals. Believe and know that satisfaction is the only possibility. Don't worry about what other people think about your sticking to impossible ideas. They may not know what you know. Defy your programming and especially the world's programming that says it is a dog-eat-dog world. Know that the Universe is for you always. Refuse to feel sorry for yourself, because you are a winner and you are determined to experience nothing but victory.

10. Dare to feel good about yourself. Yes, feel good about yourself even before you've demonstrated all the things you've been working to achieve. Don't depend on other people to make you feel good. Yes, they can make you feel good, but you don't need their congratulations or their approval. You walk your own path and are creating a unique experience of life. You know when you've done well, so tell yourself that you did well.

If people criticize what you've done, if there's something to learn from it, learn it, but don't allow the criticism to undermine you or stop you from doing what you know you have to do. As soon as you can, tell yourself that you will do even better tomorrow. You already have within you everything you could possibly need to demonstrate your satisfaction, your goals and your prosperity.

GO FOR MORE

Do you wish to have more of the good things in life? Sure you do. But maybe you've grown accustomed to having less. Surely you've noticed how hard people work for more good and perhaps it exhausts you to watch. You also see how chaotic their lives are when they do move up in the world, buy a bigger and better house and take on a more responsible job. Changes occur and changes are sometimes unpleasant or even scary because you're dealing with the unknown.

If you would like to have more and expect to have more, you must expect changes to happen. If you don't wish to experience all the changes that having more prosperity entails, then why treat for or affirm that you are prosperous? Having more good means more responsibility. Ask yourself if you are willing to be responsible for the conditions that more prosperity brings.

Everyone has the potential to be prosperous. Everyone deserves prosperity because of who and what they are. But not all people will be prosperous. Why not? Well, it's certainly not God's fault. God doesn't care who's rich or even who's poor. Everyone came to Planet Earth equipped with all the spiritual power necessary to reach for the skies, and can be, do or have anything they can imagine. Most of us, however, will not use that equipment in a very big way. Why not? The answer is that we will not discipline ourselves to think in a way that creates prosperity. It is as simple as that.

IT'S TIME TO TALK ABOUT MONEY

Prosperity includes money, but it's much more than money. People generally entertain some interesting ideas about money.

Do you believe that money is bad? Many people criticize the students of Science of Mind for talking too much about money. Traditional thinking is that money is the cause of all kinds of problems, among them, crime and family feuds. They say that money is the root of all evil. But is money evil?

Mark Twain said that the *lack* of money is the root of all evil. Poverty thinking and not understanding that there is law supporting our thinking create wrong action. Not understanding that everyone is potentially powerful, people believe they have to steal and kill for money to buy what they think they need. Money, again, is not the cause. It is people's motives, their thinking and the actions they take that cause negative consequences.

What is money? Money is neutral. It is simply a unit of value. The government has printed some paper, minted some coins and assigned values to them so that we, the people, can exchange them for food, clothing and shelter. At present a loaf of bread requires exchange units valued at $4.49. We pay $3.75 for a half-gallon of milk. It takes many units of exchange to buy food these days, if you've noticed.

The great thing about money is it's portable and easy to store. My grandmother used to exchange chickens for provisions. Unlike chickens, you can keep money in your pocket. Chickens are awkward to carry. They aren't convenient or portable. It's next to impossible to keep a chicken in your pocket and hold onto it until you exchange it for a gallon of milk at Ralph's. Money just makes shopping easier.

Another good thing about money is if you have some left over, you can lend it to someone and charge interest for it and increase your supply of exchange units.

Do you have all the money you require or do you feel poor? If you feel you never have enough money, how do you begin to change your consciousness from lack to plenty? Where do you start? You start by declaring you have plenty of money.? What if you don't believe that?

Ernest Holmes wrote: "Since we must begin right where we are, most of us will be compelled to begin our healing work with a mechanical process."

This means we must start with our unbelief. The belief is that we cannot have more. But to go for more, he instructs us: "We should take the highest thought we have, and attempt to enlarge on this consciousness until it embraces a more vital concept of reality."

What does he mean? He means that if we change the thought "I don't have" to a higher thought, such as, "I have all I require," and think about it, begin to believe in it, we will start to build the idea "I have all I require" into consciousness. When you begin to affirm, you may not have any feeling at all for that higher thought, but if you keep thinking about it, seeing it and imagining it, feeling will come. That idea will become infused with life.

And he also tells us what consciousness is: "Consciousness in this sense means an inner embodiment of ideas." What does embodiment mean? It means that we begin to think from and react from an idea. As we work with an idea, it becomes filled with meaning and feeling. We begin to believe in our idea.

Ernest also says: "If one wishes to demonstrate prosperity, he must first have a consciousness of prosperity. This is more than faith; it is the knowledge that we are dealing with Law." We are dealing with how life works at its essence. He concludes with: "While a certain consciousness may be mechanically induced, of course, the more spontaneity put into the mechanical word, the more power the word must have."

We may affirm that we are millionaires until we are blue in the face, and never believe we can become millionaires. Why? Because most of us don't believe we have the talent or the skills or the knowledge to make a fortune. Another reason we think we can't be millionaires is that we *don't know* how *it can happen.* This is a mental block to having more.

But it is possible to imagine a little more than we have now and become more affluent.

What does *affluent* mean? It means being in the flow of abundance, that your good is flowing copiously. Being affluent means that there's good behind you and good ahead of you. There is no blockage. This fits with my definition of prosperity. It's being free to do what you wish whenever you wish, and feeling at peace with yourself.

Affluence is an affirmative state of living, a constructive outlook on the world. If this becomes our major view, we will eventually become prosperous.

Maybe you've reached the point where you're saying, "Okay, okay, I get it. Now just tell me what I have to do to go for more."

DEVELOPING A PROSPERITY CONSCIOUSNESS

We've talked about factors for creating prosperity and we've talked about essential thought patterns to create. Now let's talk about some ideas in which we also need to develop trust in order to build that consciousness of prosperity.

1. All is Mind and the action of Mind. Everything we are, everything we think, see and experience is Mind in action, Mind expressing Itself.

Why is this important to know? Infinite Mind, the Mind of Spirit, is the only Mind and the one we think with. Mind creates thoughts. Thoughts are the result of thinking. Mind and Its Law respond to our thoughts and create something out of them.

Imagine thought as a nucleus around which other thoughts gather. A nucleus gathers thought-substance and a form begins to appear. Thoughts have substance.

2. Use denial constructively. Take a look at the way you think generally. You have a trend of thinking and that trend reveals itself as the condition of your life. Look at your life and you will see how you've been thinking.

If you discover that you've been thinking against your own best interests, decide to change the trend of your thinking. Resolve to *deny* thoughts that are unproductive, negative or detrimental to your progress. Those thoughts are denying you your right to go for more. They are keeping you in lack. Denials, used in the correct way, are powerful. Denials are not refusing to face reality. Use them to erase something you no longer wish to experience. Clear the way to create what you do wish to experience.

3. Speak to yourself in a constructive way. For instance: When there's something expensive that you would like, do you say, "I can't afford that"? Tell yourself instead: "I can afford that at the perfect right time in a perfect way." If you must buy a cheaper version, say, "I choose to buy this at this time."

4. Your thoughts create your life. Begin to cultivate a fresh outlook on life. Start looking for the beautiful, the good, the whole, the free and things that promote life and love and joy.

Acknowledge them and know that you are one with all you see. This is why you wish to see spiritual qualities. Appreciate them. Appreciation spurs things to grow. You are a part of the grandeur, beauty and abundance of the Universe. Appreciate your life, your family, your friends and your work. See the good in everything and everyone.

5. Shake up your routine. Court new ideas, fresh ideas, bigger ideas. Do things differently so that you are compelled to think before you do something. When you have to think, you don't follow the crowd or just go with the flow, in particular when it's negative. You have to be creative. This takes alertness on your part.

6. Dare to make plans. Plan definitely to do something that you think you can't afford to do right now. Your definite resolve to have some particular experience sets the Universe to work specifically for you.

A few years ago, I read an article on Charleston, South Carolina, in the travel section of the *LA Times*. I enjoyed very much what I read and the pictures accompanying the article captivated me. I suddenly wanted to go there, sightsee, enjoy the cuisine and spend a little time getting acquainted with the city. I didn't have extra money to travel, but I made a decision to go. It was a firm decision. I didn't realize it, but as soon as I made the decision, behind the scenes, the Universe began arranging for that to happen.

Not long after making my decision, I attended a charity event and met a woman with whom I became friends. Not many months later, my new friend and her husband bought a plantation near Charleston. That summer, she invited me to come and stay with her in Charleston for a long weekend. Her husband's business represented an airline and he gave us first-class plane tickets. We rode horses on the plantation, ate delicious regional fare and explored the city of Charleston. It was every bit as wonderful as I had thought it would be. Several years in a row I was invited to visit my friend and grew to know and love Charleston.

It took very little money to realize my dream. I simply made the decision to go there, and the rest unfolded like magic.

The Law of Mind cannot create anything from vague thoughts and ideas. Vague thoughts are not cohesive. They have no nucleus to attract substance. The law works with definite ideas and feelings. Affirm your plans. Visualize them. Tell yourself they are now taking shape and are unfolding at exactly the right time.

So, make plans and watch them happen!

7. Train yourself to think prosperously. To court a prosperity consciousness, there are some actions you can take to enhance your thoughts and feelings. The Law reflects back to you the general state of your consciousness. Feel prosperous. Speak prosperity. Dress as if you were prosperous and act as if you were prosperous. You will soon experience prosperity.

To cultivate a prosperous outlook, old-time adherents of New Thought instructed you to go sit in a bank and watch money being exchanged. Go to the best shops that sell the best clothes, choose something you love, try it on and plan to have it.

8. Be lavish in your ability to forgive. Forgiveness is generosity and largeness of Spirit. Be outrageously generous.

I know of a relationship between two friends that was ruined by a disagreement. Neither was willing to step up and forgive the other, nor ask for forgiveness. John didn't think he had done anything wrong to Doug. Doug believed that John had done him wrong. Neither would budge. The anger and distrust between them festered and grew poisonous. To date, they've not spoken to each other for two years. I know and like both of these men. When I mention one to the other, I can see the anger rise. Needless to say, neither one is flourishing at the present.

Hatred and resentment diminish everyone. These caustic emotions tend to depress your immune system, which may eventually invite disease. Be the first one to forgive. Even if you think it's not your fault, say, "If I did something to hurt you, I'm sorry. Please forgive me." You may not have done anything to hurt someone, but they may believe you did.

9. Let it flow. Anything that is not moving is dead. Everything alive moves forward. If your life is not moving forward, check your pulse.

Actually, just as your body is never the same body from moment to moment, everything – because it's all God – is dancing with life. Your good is always present. Supply is all around you, within you.

How is this so? The Law of Circulation.

Earlier I said there is no such thing as supply and demand. In Science of Mind, it's demand and supply. When you make a demand, the supply is furnished.

If we tell ourselves that we require money for our rent by tomorrow, we must be definite about it. We may not have the least idea where it's coming from. But we must have the courage to stand up and demand that the Universe supply it. The Universe is the source of all, the channels through which our supply flows.

You experience good to the degree that you are willing to allow "the creative current" to flow through you. Life is designed to flow. Life is Spirit, forever flowing in and through everything. When you're afraid — let's say afraid of not having enough or not meeting a bill — you become tense. Your circulation becomes restricted. If this goes on long enough you may create a condition called hypertension. But when you relax, your circulation becomes normal.

It's the same with supply. Relax, make your demand and then allow your good to flow in and allow it to flow out. Giving and receiving are all one. It's the same stream of good. Don't be afraid to give. Give to your source of inspiration. Give to organizations and people who inspire you. Give only if it makes you feel good, if it makes you feel prosperous. Don't give if you are afraid. Talk yourself out of being afraid. Relax and open yourself up to giving more so that you will receive more. Don't give just to receive, however; give to have the pleasure of giving. It is certain that what you give will come back.

Another way to give is to let go of things you no longer need. Order and balance are qualities of God. If you hold onto things, your life may become cluttered and disorderly. Give away things you're not using. Make room for newer and better in every area of your life.

10. Declare that you are governed totally by the Law of Divine Right Action. Divine Right Action is the action of Spirit and Its Law. It is the highest and the best. Everything comes to you at just the right time, just as you require it. When life works like this, you are in the flow of affluence and echoing the actions of the only Cause and Creator. When you speak into the Law with definiteness, you are speaking with the authority and power of the Universe.

Why are you able to do this? Because you now know that life works by Law and it works for you, just as if there were no other person in the world. It is waiting for you to command it into action and into manifestation.

Get busy. Don't wait another day to move beyond wealth into a prosperity consciousness. You have always had the power and ability to go for more. You can do it now...

...the Science of Mind way.

CHAPTER 3

Recipe for Love
Creating Better Relationships

———————

We all have seen beautiful and loving relationships, yet we have also seen unhappy relationships that end sadly. Knowing it's possible for love to last forever, how do we start and build a loving relationship with so many fears spinning around in our heads?

Everyone wants love. Everyone wants to be loved. But how many people are willing to be the first to actually express love? Are you?

Arthur Rubinstein, the great pianist, once said, "Love life and life will love you back. Love people and they will love you back." There is some truth to this, but in today's world you will most certainly find someone who disagrees. Can it really be that simple, to just give love and expect love in return? Most of us are neither ready nor willing to do that. In this chapter we'll talk about love, the Science of Mind way.

When we love, we see through the eyes of love. Neville, a New Thought writer and lecturer, wrote: "People are what you choose to make them; a man is according to the manner in which you look at him. You must look at him with different eyes before he will objectively change." In other words, people are what we see them to be and what we decide they are. We can only know them by way of our consciousness; we see them through our attitude about life and people. We see them through what we believe people to be.

We can never know people as they know themselves. They become to us what we think they are. In reality, the only relationship we ever have is with ourselves. That means we can have a loving and respectful relationship with anyone – provided we have a loving and respectful relationship with ourselves. Conversely, if we don't like ourselves, if we think we are flawed human beings, it is likely that we will look out on the world and see flawed people everywhere.

SELF-LOVE CONSCIOUSNESS

Loving yourself is imperative if you wish to have a healthy, loving relationship with another person. If you don't already love yourself, find out what's holding you back. On one hand, some people try to keep a distance from a relationship. They prevent others from getting close for all kinds of reasons. Perhaps it's because something in them knows that they will see themselves if they get "too" close. Or perhaps, since they don't know who they are yet, they believe they don't deserve a partner.

Learn to love yourself. You can start by looking inward and identifying why your consciousness (belief system) is discouraging love from entering your life. For some, this may require professional assistance. For others, it may take just a pep talk from a dear friend. Either way, work to overcome those barriers.

Loving ourselves, for many of us, is a process. We have to grow into the ability to love and respect ourselves. When we understand our true identity as individualized expressions of Spirit, it becomes easier to love and respect ourselves. Out of this understanding grows the ability to love and respect others, because they too, have a Divine Identity. Our relationships improve as a natural result.

Barbara De Angelis, New Thought minister and teacher, says, "If you aren't good at loving yourself, you will have a difficult time loving anyone, since you'll resent the time and energy you give another person that you aren't even giving to yourself."

The Science of Mind teaches that God is Love. We are God individualized. That means we embody Love. Love is our true nature. It will always be there. But love may not have been expressed in some of us. We have to grow into our ability to express and to give – and even to receive – love.

Why is this? When we arrive here as babies, we are completely self-involved. As our mother takes care of us, feeds us, cuddles us, makes us feel secure, we begin to love her as someone to depend on, someone who's always there. Now we have begun to expand beyond the self and look outward to love someone else "out there." We may then learn to love our father, our siblings, our relatives and friends, our teachers and mentors. Then we meet a special person and fall in love, a new and exciting love like nothing else before.

Now we are ready for a higher, more satisfying and intimate relationship with another person. *The Science of Mind* teaches us that as spiritual beings, we are always connected to Source Power, to Love, to Infinite Mind and all its wisdom and intelligence and knowledge – as well as to every living being in the Universe.

Our capacity to love is expanding all the time. If we express it, we grow more adept at expressing it, and as the Principle of Life works, it reflects back to us what we have in our hearts, what we are thinking. If we express lots of love, love comes back to us lavishly. When we've expanded our capacity to love the world generally, it is usually because we have become a self-realized and spiritually aware being.

All the learning and growing we do spiritually is in awareness of our Divine identity and what that potentially means to us. Some of us, of course, never learn who we truly are. Some know it intuitively and act on it. But some of us, because we don't know who we are, never develop a good relationship with ourselves. That usually means that we don't have satisfying relationships with people in general. People come and go in our lives, leaving us devastated, and we don't know why our relationships don't last.

We don't realize that each person that passes through our life or remains in our life is a reflection of how we feel about ourselves. If we've learned how to love from our family relationships, or we've taken the time to learn how to love and give, then we begin to realize that all loving and giving starts right here at the door of our own consciousness.

In the final analysis, life, for me, is all about me. Life for you is all about you. That puts each one of us in the driver's seat of our life and our ability to express love. Life will be what we make it. And we will be loved if we learn how to love.

LEARNING HOW TO LOVE

Once we have reached a consciousness of self-love, we are able to give and receive. One way to develop and express our ability to love is through relationships, friendly or intimate ones.

Generally, relationships have to be created; they rarely just happen. To create the highest form of relationship, it would be good to be aware of our own assets and maybe even what we consider our liabilities. As opportunities come and go, it's important to remember that relationships mirror back to us our beliefs about life and people. Establishing a spiritual relationship requires awareness of who we are, what we like and what we expect from people with whom we are going to be intimate.

The first thing to realize is that every person is already whole. This means everyone is whole, both the aware and the unaware. No one needs a relationship to complete him or her. Two halves – when it comes to people – do not make a whole.

The longing to be one with our beloved arises from the True Self that knows we are already one.

Before we even start a relationship, it might be wise to ask ourselves:

Is it naïve of me to want love?

Is my desire for personal happiness frivolous
when the world is in such bad shape?

Do I equate affection and tenderness with
sentimentality and weakness?

If someone is generous and loving to me,
should I be suspicious?

If someone hurts me, am I being weak and
foolish if I forgive them?

If I love this person enough, will it change him or her?

Is it just plain foolhardy to trust anyone with my love?

If I'm trying to be loving, giving, forgiving, generous and
trusting, am I being a big phony?

If the answer is "yes" to many of these questions, we do not
truly know ourselves. If we don't truly know who we are, we
don't know who anyone else is. How can we trust anyone if we
can't trust ourselves?

However, if you answered "no" to most of these questions, it
indicates that you know and trust yourself. At this point you're
strong enough to say, "I'd like to have a deeper relationship
with you, but I need to know if there's anything about me that
concerns you. Is there?"

The quality of the answer will reveal the future of your
relationship with him or her. The person who loves you will say

something like this: "You don't have to give up anything. You can do anything you like. You can be anything you like or have anything you like. I'll be here for you. I'll cheer you on."

An answer like that is the one we ought to have. In a good relationship we encourage each other to strive for the highest possible emotional, intellectual and spiritual growth.

HEALTHY RELATIONSHIPS

A healthy relationship is created when two whole, loving, compassionate, tender and joyful people come together in love. The loving spiritual partnership that they create, through synergy, becomes even more powerful and fulfilling. The partnership becomes something even greater than either one alone would be.

A loving relationship begins when we develop our capacity to love and to give without conditions on how much love we give. As we love, our capacity to love and give love increases. A partnership offers us the opportunity to grow even more able to love. We have someone to give to, to share with, to celebrate our victories with, but also to comfort us when we are hurt. When we are going through trying times, it's a great comfort to have someone beside us, helping us to get through these hardships with tenderness and compassion.

Sometimes, a loving relationship demands that one person do all the loving for a time. This is what frightens some of us the most: What if I give and give and love and love and they don't give anything back to me? Does that leave me out in the cold? A loving, spiritual partner never withholds love, never counts and measures how much love he or she is giving to the other one who is suffering.

Love never abandons you. Loving creates an opportunity for you to grow even more in your ability to love. You are enriching yourself when you love. The person who continues to love is the biggest beneficiary in the long run. How does that Beatles song go? "…And in the end, the love you take is equal to the love you make."

There's no such thing as giving too much love. If we withhold love, we are only withholding love from ourselves. If we wish to have a loving relationship, we start by giving love. It begins there. A relationship requires more, of course. It requires that we develop in ourselves the qualities we admire in other people.

What we have, we can give. If we don't have it, we can't give it. For instance, if that person with whom we are developing a relationship has some quality that we believe we don't have, we may think that by loving that person, that quality will somehow belong to us. In reality, if you admire a quality, it must already be in you. Latent, perhaps, but awakened simply by the recognition of it in another. Recognizing a good quality in another awakens the same in us and gives us the opportunity to bring it out and express it.

Some people fall in love with certain good qualities the beloved possesses. If they don't like a quality the person possesses, they believe that love will change that person and he or she will lose that quality. However, that probably won't happen. By the same token, we don't need to change ourselves to earn someone's love. Doing so rarely works anyway. If we were spiritually aware, it would serve to increase our capacity to see spiritual qualities in our beloved, to keep looking for those qualities and to keep them always in sight. By looking beyond surface attributes and sexual attraction, we can recognize the Spiritual Perfection that all of us possess. Spiritually aware people know that deep down we are all connected. An intimate and even sexual relationship at its best expresses that unity and connection we all share.

Yes, all of us desire a loving relationship with a compatible soul. Ask anyone who lives alone. Whether we are nineteen or ninety, we desire to experience intimacy and closeness in all kinds of ways. We wish to have a relationship that expresses on all levels, from sexual to platonic.

Why? Because a relationship is a way to get to know ourselves better. We are seeing ourselves in that relationship. That person is in reality mirroring back to us our beliefs and attitudes, whether we love ourselves or not. It's wonderful to see yourself reflected back as love.

UNHEALTHY RELATIONSHIPS

We are perfect in our Essence, but not as a human. No one on this earth is a perfect person – even a spiritually aware one – and from time to time, unhealthy thoughts and actions creep into our lives, causing us to shift the focus of our relationship from love-based to one based on fear. This can have harmful effects.

If a relationship endangers our human dignity, prevents us from growing in necessary ways, if it depresses us or demoralizes us, you can be sure it's not a healthy one and it's not right for us.

Emotional ultimatums, with terms and conditions, can be toxic to a relationship. What if your beloved demands that you see only each other and forget about all other relationships? Is that love? No, it's called possession. The secure partner releases his or her loved one to perfect freedom. If we love people in a healthy way, we wish them to be free. When we spend time with our beloved, attentive to their presence, seeing and hearing them, we don't have to worry about them when they leave our sight. Healthy, confident people trust each other.

A spiritually aware person realizes that choices are vital to a rich and healthy life. When we shove emotional ultimatums on our loved ones, we are essentially attempting to relieve them of their right to make choices. In order for the relationship to grow, it depends on the growth of each person without the use of emotional ultimatums. Be cautious when you or your partner start placing terms and conditions on the relationship. If it happens, it's perfectly acceptable to question someone's love, especially if it depends on asking a partner to change something about him or herself.

Relationships change; they go through trials. Sometimes these periods are the impetus for us to grow the most. But in all cases, we need to feel safe enough with our partner to talk out our problems with each other. Love is feeling secure to safely express ourselves. If we talk out our problems without arguing, we can release the hurt and become even closer. Not dealing with our feelings and issues robs us of the love and trust we desire with each other.

That's not to say that in a perfectly wonderful relationship people won't have disagreements and even arguments. There are times when we feel hurt by our loved ones. Or we resent them. We may, in the heat of emotion, impulsively blurt out things that are not true, or maybe they say things so true we'd rather not hear them.

When we repress our feelings, they can play havoc with our health and certainly with our relationships. Feelings need to be dealt with, not repressed. Suppressed feelings lie in our subconscious mind and once there, they fester and ferment and subtly poison our outlook on life. So don't be afraid to express your feelings.

By dealing with things as soon as possible, we are not sitting around brooding and feeling sorry for ourselves, allowing our differences to become a wall between us.

If we respect and love ourselves, we will not become a

doormat and allow the other to walk all over us simply to keep their love. Why would anyone become a doormat? Because of the fear of losing the loved one. If we don't know who we are, we may fear losing that special person because we believe we won't be complete without them.

However, if you're afraid your partner will walk out if you express any of your feelings, you've allowed your right of choice to be taken from you. Even if that special person chooses to walk out and never return, an aware person knows he or she will still be complete.

What if your beloved criticizes you? We all have faults. We all have habits that might be annoying to someone else. The person who loves you has obviously decided that he or she loves you in spite of your faults. But what if they point out your faults? Be open-minded enough to listen. If your mate has a point, think about it. Is it valid? Do you need to do something about it? If you think you don't, then tell your mate you don't think you'll do anything about it. Then don't worry about it.

Worry eats at a relationship. Worry is planning for the worst to happen. If you worry that your beloved is going to leave you because you don't deserve him or her, eventually they may indeed leave. Not because you don't deserve them, but because you think, say and do things that reinforce your partner's belief that you're not worth the trouble. He or she may be persuaded – by you – to agree with you.

But it won't be the truth. You are worthy of all good. You always were, whether you knew it or not. You deserve the very highest and best, not because of what you do or say, but because of who you are: a spiritual being, an individualization of Love Itself.

THE ESSENCE OF LOVE

A spiritually aware person knows from the get-go that they are complete at their Essence. When we know who we are and love ourselves as we are, we have the courage to speak up and express ourselves, even our strongest feelings. All positive feelings have constructive effects.

In a spiritual partnership we recognize that no one is better than we are and no one is less than we are. Everyone is endowed with different talents and qualities. But each unique expression of the Divine is whole and complete. Feel free to express love, tenderness, compassion, understanding and joy.

Remember:

- You can only know people through your consciousness.
- You are the creator of all relationships.
- As a spiritually aware person, you have no fear of loving and giving.
- You are functioning in this relationship with great self-worth, always growing in your capacity to give love and to receive love.
- You are happy and fulfilled and are able to sail on even in the face of problems and strongly expressed feelings.
- Have fun in life! Do zany, crazy things sometimes and never be afraid of being laughed at.

Your beloved may be a part of your life right now, or just around the next corner. Either way, remember that all loving relationships are connected with the Universe, based in loved and built upon trust.

Life is grand when we love. It's grand when we can live and speak the truth through love. And when we love, we experience life in the highest and best way possible...

...the Science of Mind way.

About the Author

JOAN McCALL began her spiritual quest in earnest in her early twenties. While she pursued an acting career, she continued to study metaphysics deeply. These studies led her to train and become a licensed practitioner of the Science of Mind and an ordained minister of Religious Science. She taught Science of Mind classes for five years and founded the Creative Arts Center for Spiritual Living in Los Angeles, where she taught and spoke for another five years.

It is certain that her spiritual studies benefited her career. Joan's first two jobs in her chosen profession were leading roles on Broadway, followed immediately by starring roles in two national tours. In Hollywood she landed leading roles in two movies. Not thrilled with the quality of roles she was offered, she wrote a screenplay that established herself as a staff writer on *Days of Our Lives*, a daytime television series.

Joan also wrote more than a hundred television episodes for *Another World*.

Joan and her husband, film producer David Sheldon wrote a screenplay sequel to his production of *Grizzly* that was filmed in Hungary and starred Deborah Raffin, George Clooney, Charlie Sheen and Laura Dern. They co-authored the book *When I Knew Al: The Untold Story of Al Pacino*, published in 2006.

Joan and David live in Los Angeles, where they have a motion picture production company and write screenplays together for independent producers.